Le Cordon Bleu

Techniques and Recipes
Pastry, Cakes
& Biscuits

LE CORDON BLEU

TECHNIQUES AND RECIPES
PASTRY, CAKES
& BISCUITS

JENI WRIGHT AND ERIC TREUILLE

CASSELL

A CASSELL BOOK

This edition first published in the United Kingdom in 1998 by
Cassell plc
Wellington House
125 Strand
London WC2R 0BB

Created and Produced by
CARROLL & BROWN LIMITED
20 Lonsdale Road
London NW6 6RD

Material in this book has been previously published in
Le Cordon Bleu Complete Cooking Techniques
published by Cassell at £25

British Library Catalogue-in-Publication Data
A catalogue record for this book is available from the
British Library

ISBN 0-304-35126-1

Reproduced by Colourscan, Singapore
Printed and bound in Great Britain by Jarrold Book Printing,
Thetford, Norfolk

CONTENTS

SHORTCRUST PASTRY

A rich, flaky dough, shortcrust pastry is the simplest, most versatile pastry. Called *pâte brisée* in French, it is used for flans, tarts and quiches, and for single and double crust pies. It is also ideal for tartlet shells, and for decorative finishes. If sugar is added, it is called *pâte sucrée*.

PATE BRISEE AND PATE SUCREE

200 g plain flour, sifted
I tsp salt
100 g unsalted butter, diced
I egg
About 2 tsp water

Mix flour and salt. Rub in butter. Add egg and enough water to make a dough. Wrap and chill, 30 minutes. Makes 400 g.

For *pâte sucrée*, add I tbsp caster sugar with the salt.

TRICK OF THE TRADE

USING A PASTRY BLENDER

English shortcrust pastry is slightly different from French *pâte brisée*. Traditionally it is made with equal quantities of butter and lard to double the amount of flour. A special tool, called a pastry blender, with sharp steel wires attached to a handle, is good for cutting in the fat and aerating it at the same time.

MAKING PATE BRISEE

Pâte brisée for savoury dishes, and pâte sucrée for desserts, use identical techniques. For best results, keep utensils and ingredients cool and handle the dough as little as possible. Once worked into a ball, refrigerate dough for 30 minutes to allow it to relax – this helps prevent shrinkage during baking.

1 Sift flour through a fine sieve into a large bowl. This will aerate the dough and help make the finished pastry crisp and light. Stir in salt.

2 Rub the butter in with your fingers until the mixture is even in colour and resembles fine breadcrumbs.

3 Shake the bowl to ensure all the butter has been incorporated, then make a well in the centre.

4 Lightly beat the egg in a separate small bowl, then pour it into the well.

5 Work the mixture with a pastry scraper, adding water as necessary, about 1 tsp at a time, until the dough begins to hold together.

6 Bring the dough together with your hand, then put it on the work surface and shape into a rough ball. Do not overwork the dough or the pastry will be tough.

LINING A FLAN TIN

To prevent baked pastry shrinking, take care not to stretch the dough when rolling it out and fitting it into the tin, and chill the shell for at least 30 minutes.

1 Roll dough to a round 5 cm larger than tin and wrap around rolling pin. Unroll loosely over tin.

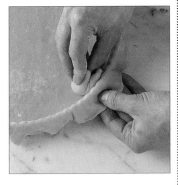

2 Use a small ball of excess dough to press the dough over the bottom and into the seam of the tin.

3 Roll the rolling pin over the top of the tin, pressing down firmly with your hand to cut off excess dough.

BAKING BLIND

Pastry shells for flans, quiches, tarts and tartlets need to be fully baked if the filling does not need to be cooked, or partially baked if the cooking time for the filling is short. The technique of baking an empty shell is called "baking blind".

1 Prick bottom of shell to allow trapped air to escape during baking. Line with parchment, fill with baking beans and bake at 180°C, 10–15 minutes.

2 When pastry is set and rim is golden, remove paper and beans and bake for a further 5 minutes or until lightly browned. Let cool on a wire rack.

MAKING TARTLETS

When baking small pastry shells blind, it is easier to weight them down with another mould placed on top of the pastry than to fill individual moulds with paper and baking beans.

1 Line a tartlet mould with dough; trim. Place another mould inside; press gently to secure. Bake at 180°C, 10 minutes. Remove top mould and bake a further 5 minutes until lightly browned.

2 Unmould and let cool on a wire rack. Fill with crème pâtissière (see page 39), top with fresh fruits and brush with fruit glaze (see page 31).

(see page 39), ... (see page 31).

BAKING BEANS

When pastry is baked blind – without a filling – it must be held in place by weights to prevent it rising and bubbling up. Place a piece of baking parchment over the bottom, slightly larger than the tin. Fill with an even layer of baking beans – these can be the commercially made china or metal variety, or dried beans or rice, all of which can be re-used.

PIE FUNNELS

Funnels help support pastry and allow steam to escape. Use a decorative ceramic type, often made in the shape of a bird, or a homemade foil one.

MAKING A SINGLE CRUST PIE

Deep-dish sweet and savoury pies are generally covered with a single, top crust of shortcrust pastry. To ensure the pastry remains secure and does not fall into the filling during cooking, a double collar of dough is made around the edge. For added stability, a pie funnel (see box, left), is set in the centre of the filling to act as a support for the pastry.

1 Roll out dough 2.5–5 cm larger than the dish. Place dish upside-down in the centre. Cut around edge of dish. Cut out a 2-cm collar from the excess dough.

2 Spoon cold filling around funnel. Moisten rim of dish with a pastry brush dipped in water and press on the collar of dough. Brush the collar with water.

3 Wrap lid over rolling pin and carefully unroll over top of dish. Press on to collar. Trim excess dough by running a knife blade around the edge of the dish.

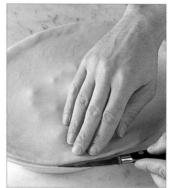

4 "Knock-up" by lightly pressing the rim with your fingers and tapping the back of the knife blade around the edges of the dough to create ridges.

5 Press thumb on rim; draw back a floured knife 1 cm towards centre. Repeat around pie. Cut a hole over funnel, brush lid with egg wash (see page 43).

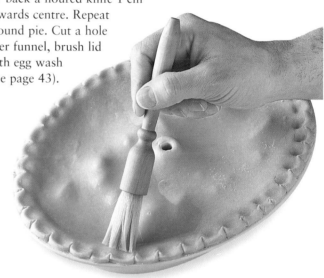

MAKING A DOUBLE CRUST PIE

Pies made in shallow dishes or pie plates are often baked with a double crust of pastry – one underneath the filling and another on top. To prevent the bottom layer becoming soggy, brush it with a little lightly whisked egg white before filling, and use a fruit that is firm and not over juicy, such as the rhubarb shown here.

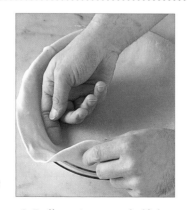

1 Roll out just over half the dough and lay it in the dish. Using the back of your finger, press the dough into the dish; be careful not to stretch it. Trim excess.

2 Spoon in cold filling. Roll out remaining dough slightly larger than dish and wrap around rolling pin. Moisten rim, then unroll dough over filling. Trim and knock-up edges, make steam vents in lid, then glaze (see step 5, above).

DECORATIVE EDGES

Tarts and pies of all types benefit from a prettily shaped edging, or a pastry decoration made from trimmings or an additional sheet of dough. These can be added to the outer edge of the pie or applied as a top crust. Flour your fingers to make the dough easy to handle, and apply an egg wash glaze (see page 43) before baking.

FLUTES
Place one forefinger and thumb inside edge of dough. Pinch between them; sharpen the shape by pinching with your other forefinger and thumb.

LEAVES
Cut out leaves from trimmings. Make veins by lightly scoring the dough with the tip of a knife. Moisten rim and press on leaves, overlapping them slightly.

PLAIT
Cut three 1-cm wide strips of dough, about 5 cm longer than the circumference of the dish. Place strips side by side and plait. Brush rim of dough with water and place plait around rim; press lightly to secure and join ends.

LATTICE
Cut 1.5-cm wide strips. Lay across tart, 2 cm apart. Fold back alternate strips until 2 cm from rim and lay a new strip horizontally across the others. Reverse the folded and unfolded strips. Repeat at 2 cm intervals.

ROSE
Make a 2-cm cone of dough. Cut out five 3-cm rounds for petals. Press your thumb on part of each petal to make it flat. Wrap flat edge around cone; pinch to secure. Repeat, working around cone and overlapping petals slightly.

TARTE TATIN

This classic French dessert is cooked under a pastry lid, then served upside-down.

1 Roll out shortcrust dough to a round slightly larger than pan. Place over fruit and trim off excess. Tuck in edges. Bake at 230°C, 20 minutes.

2 Let rest 10 minutes, then place serving plate on top of pan and invert. Carefully remove pan.

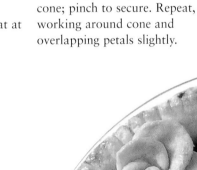

CHOUX PASTRY

Creating the crisp, airy shells for buns and eclairs, dazzling desserts like croquembouche (see page 12) and many savoury hors d'oeuvre, *pâte à choux*, a dough that is cooked twice, is unlike any other pastry.

CHOUX PASTE

The essential technique is to cook the paste until it begins to puff up, then add the eggs very slowly off the heat, beating to incorporate as much air as possible. The paste should be just warm enough to cook the eggs slightly but not so hot that it sets the mixture. This quantity of choux paste will make 40 buns (see below) or 30 eclairs (see opposite page).

1 Bring 100 g unsalted butter and 250 ml water just to the boil; remove the pan from the heat.

2 Add 150 g plain flour sifted with 1 tsp each salt and sugar and beat.

3 When dough is smooth, return to heat until it is dry, forms a ball and pulls away from the side of the pan.

4 Slowly add four beaten eggs, off the heat so they do not cook, beating well after each addition.

5 Continue beating until paste is thick and shiny. It should drop off spoon when shaken.

CHOUX BUNS

These small balls of choux paste are piped, baked, then cooled and either cut in half and sandwiched together again with a filling, or pierced in the bottom and piped with a filling (see box, opposite page). Before baking, lightly butter baking sheets and chill in the refrigerator – so the mixture will not slip when piped. Bake at 200°C, until golden, about 20 minutes.

1 Pipe mounds on buttered baking sheet with 1-cm plain nozzle; space well apart.

2 Lightly brush tops with a small amount of egg wash (see page 43).

3 Slightly flatten balls with a fork dipped in egg wash to form rounded top.

ECLAIRS

Choux paste is piped into 8-cm lengths for eclairs. Use a 1-cm plain nozzle and space them apart on chilled, lightly buttered baking sheets. Bake at 200°C for 20–25 minutes until golden brown, then cool on a rack. Here eclairs are pierced and piped with crème pâtissière (see page 39) flavoured with melted couverture chocolate. For other fillings, see box, right.

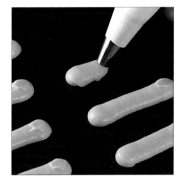

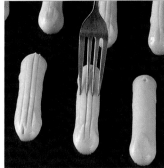

1 Pipe choux directly on to baking sheet, applying even pressure to keep shapes as uniform as possible.

2 Brush the choux fingers with egg wash (see page 43) and score with a fork dipped in egg wash.

3 Let eclairs cool on rack. When ready to fill, pierce eclairs at each end with tip of small knife or piping nozzle.

4 Pipe filling into one of the holes with a 5-mm nozzle. Stop piping when filling starts to come out of the other hole.

5 Dip into softened fondant icing or tempered couverture of chocolate; remove excess.

SERVING CHOUX BUNS

- Sandwich split choux buns with piped crème Chantilly and sliced fresh fruits. Dust tops with icing sugar.

- Present choux buns with a caramel topping. Place almond slivers on a buttered baking sheet. Make caramel. Dip the top of each choux bun in the caramel, then place caramel-side down on top of an almond. Leave to set.

- Make chocolate profiteroles by filling choux buns with ice cream or crème Chantilly, then drizzling over hot chocolate sauce or melted couverture.

- Fill choux buns with piped crème mousseline and use to make croquembouche (see page 12).

- Pipe patterns on top of fondant and tempered chocolate icing. Use melted chocolate or glacé icing and pipe from a paper piping bag.

TRICK OF THE TRADE

DEEP-FRYING CHOUX

Examples of deep-fried doughs include Mexican churros, New Orleans beignets, and Italian cenci. When cooked in the same way, choux paste gives similar results. Serve dusted with icing sugar or caster sugar and cinnamon.

Heat 7.5 cm oil to 190°C. Fill a piping bag fitted with a plain 1.5-cm nozzle with choux paste. Hold the bag over the hot oil and squeeze it to extrude a piece of dough about 3 cm long. Cut off the dough close to the nozzle, using a chef's knife, so the dough falls directly into the oil. Deep-fry for 3–5 minutes until puffed and golden. Remove with a slotted spoon and drain on paper towels. Serve warm.

Croquembouche

Traditionally prepared for weddings in France, this spectacular confection consists of tiers of choux buns filled with an enriched crème pâtissière and embellished with caramel. Croquembouche is straightforward to make; each element is prepared individually before the final assembly.

SERVES 20

2 kg nougatine

Nibbed sugar, to decorate

FOR THE ROYAL ICING

250 g icing sugar

1 egg white

1 tbsp lemon juice

FOR THE CHOUX BUNS

500 ml water

200 g unsalted butter

10 g salt

15 g caster sugar

300 g plain flour

8–9 eggs

FOR THE EGG WASH

1 egg

1 egg yolk

Pinch of salt

FOR THE CREME MOUSSELINE

12 egg yolks

300 g caster sugar

100 g plain flour

100 g cornflour

1.5 litres milk infused with 1 vanilla pod

200 g unsalted butter, softened

90 ml liqueur of your choice

FOR THE CARAMEL

1 kg caster sugar

200 ml water

300 g glucose

Make the nougatine and roll it out thinly. Using a 30-cm cake card as a guide, cut out a large disc of nougatine – this will be the base of the croquembouche; set the disc aside on the card. Using a 10-cm metal cutter, cut out 2 discs of nougatine and 3 quarter moons for the top.

Make royal icing (see page 30) using the ingredients listed left; pipe around the edge of the large disc (see box, below), and around the edges of the 2 small discs.

Make 100 choux buns (see page 10), using the ingredients listed left and brushing with egg wash (see page 43) before baking.

Let cool.

Make the *crème mousseline* as for *crème pâtissière* (see page 39), whisking in the butter and liqueur a little at a time at the end; let cool. Using a small plain nozzle, pipe the crème through the hole in each choux bun.

For the caramel, dissolve the sugar in the water and bring to the boil. Skim off any scum, then stir in the glucose. Lower the heat and cook, swirling the pan occasionally, until turned to a blond caramel. Plunge base of pan into iced water to cool slightly, then dip tops of buns in the caramel and place them caramel-side down on a tray

to set. Dip a few of the buns into nibbed sugar.

Cover a large cone-shaped mould with foil and oil it well. Wrap a roll of foil around the base to support the bottom tier of buns.

Arrange buns for the bottom tier: dip the sides of the buns in caramel and stick them to each other not the foil. Add the next tier of buns (see box, below). Continue building tiers; place the buns with nibbed sugar at random. Leave to harden.

Unmould croquembouche (see box, below); set it on the nougatine base and decorate the top, sticking the shapes on with caramel.

Assembling the Croquembouche

The key to success is to take your time and work with care. The assembled croquembouche should be kept in a cool place for no longer than 4–6 hours until serving time. It should not be stored in the refrigerator because the caramel will become sticky.

Using a small star nozzle, pipe a border of royal icing shells around the edge of the large nougatine base.

Arrange tiers of choux buns around the cone, sticking them side by side and to the previous tier, not to the foil.

Gently lift the croquembouche off the mould, then carefully remove the roll of foil followed by the foil lining.

USING FILO & STRUDEL

Both these doughs bake into irresistible paper-thin layers. Creating them demands speed and practice – which is why filo is normally bought ready-made. The following methods offer ways to make the most of purchased filo, plus step-by-step instructions for homemade strudel.

LAYERING FILO

In the Middle East, filo pastry is often baked in layers with a tasty filling in between. The technique is easy, as long as you keep the filo covered with a damp cloth because it dries out very quickly. Here a baklava is made with 450 g filo, 100 g melted butter and a filling of chopped nuts, sugar and cinnamon. Bake at 170°C, 1¼ hours. Coat with a honey syrup while warm.

1 Layer half the filo sheets in buttered dish, brushing melted butter over each layer. Add filling; continue layering.

2 For a rich, gooey result, make sure top layer of filo is thoroughly drenched in melted butter before baking.

3 Before baking, score top layers in a diamond pattern with a sharp knife to make filo easy to serve.

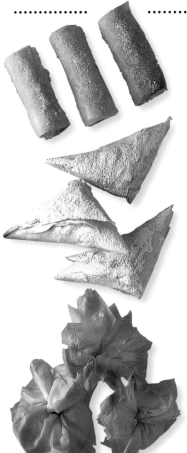

SHAPING FILO

Paper-thin filo is perfect for wrapping around fillings, sweet or savoury. As with layering (see above), keep filo covered with a damp cloth to prevent it drying out. Brush with melted butter after shaping and bake at 180°C, about 30 minutes.

CIGAR
Brush an 8-cm wide strip of filo with melted butter. Put 1 tsp filling in centre of one end. Fold over edges of the strip lengthwise to neaten. Roll up into a cigar.

TRIANGLE
Brush an 8-cm wide strip of filo with melted butter. Put 1 tsp filling in one corner of one end. Bring other corner diagonally over filling to make a triangle. Repeat folding to other end of strip.

PURSE
Brush an 8-cm square of filo with melted butter. Put 1 tsp filling in centre and gather up the corners over the filling. Twist the pastry gently just above the filling to seal without splitting the pastry.

MAKING STRUDEL

Kneading the dough thoroughly develops the gluten; letting it rest sufficiently makes it easier to stretch out. Work quickly when stretching the dough, because it dries out quickly. A simple recipe for apple strudel is given in the box, below right, using these techniques.

1 Add liquids to well in flour and quickly work into a soft ball of dough.

2 Knead dough on floured surface: pick it up and throw it down until smooth.

3 After the dough has rested, start rolling it out on a floured surface.

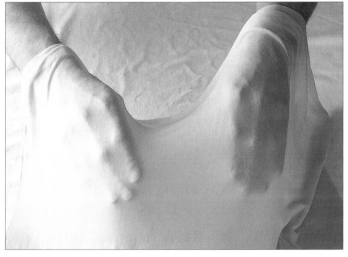

4 Working over a floured sheet, begin stretching the dough. Use the floured backs of your hands and work from the centre outwards until dough is a very thin rectangle and you can see your hands through it.

5 Sprinkle the filling over dough. Starting at one long end and using the sheet to help, roll up the dough.

6 Carefully lift the rolled strudel and place seam-side down on a buttered baking sheet. Shape into a horseshoe by curving round the ends of the roll. Brush with melted butter before baking. Serve strudel warm or cold, dusted with icing sugar and cut crosswise into thick slices. Chilled crème Chantilly (see page 19) makes a good accompaniment.

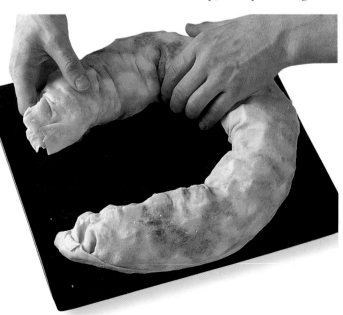

TRICK OF THE TRADE
•

LETTING DOUGH REST

When resting dough after kneading, put it in a bowl and tuck a damp tea towel around it.

APPLE STRUDEL

300 g strong plain white flour
1 tsp salt
40 ml vegetable oil
200 ml warm water
500 g cooking apples, peeled, cored and chopped
About 150 g butter, melted
150 g demerara sugar
100 g raisins
100 g walnuts, toasted and chopped
1 tsp ground cinnamon
50 g cake crumbs or fresh breadcrumbs

Sift flour and salt; add oil and water; work into ball. Knead for 5–7 minutes until smooth. Cover; let rest for up to 2 hours. Sweat apples in half the butter. Add remaining ingredients for the filling and let cool.

Roll out dough with a rolling pin, cover with a damp tea towel and let rest 15 minutes. Transfer to sheet-covered work table and stretch into a large rectangle; brush with butter. Spread filling to within 3 cm of edges. Roll up and transfer to baking sheet. Brush with butter. Bake at 190°C for 30–40 minutes. Serves 8–10.

PUFF PASTRY

There are three major stages in preparing the light, flaky and buttery pastry used for sweet and savoury tarts, bouchées and feuilletés. These are creating the *détrempe* or foundation, adding the butter, and then rolling, folding and turning the dough. For best results, keep the dough chilled.

PUFF PASTRY

500 g strong plain white flour
250 ml cold water
75 g melted unsalted butter
2 tsp salt
300 g unsalted butter

Make a dough with the flour, water, melted butter and salt. Soften the 300 g butter slightly and shape into a 2-cm thick square. Flatten dough on a lightly floured chilled surface, add the butter and enclose it in the dough. Roll, fold and turn the dough six times, chilling it in the refrigerator for 30 minutes after every second turn.
Makes 1.25 kg.

MAKING THE DETREMPE

The first stage of making the dough (détrempe in French) is working together the flour, salt, water and melted butter to the point where it forms a ball. It is then wrapped and chilled.

1 Sift flour on to chilled work surface and make a well in centre. Add water, melted butter and salt. Mix together with fingertips.

2 Using a pastry scraper, work flour-and-butter mixture until loose crumbs form. Add more water if dough becomes dry.

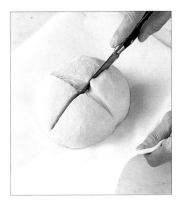

3 Shape dough into a ball. Cut an "X" on top to prevent shrinkage. Wrap dough in floured parchment; chill 30 minutes.

ADDING THE BUTTER

Before incorporating the butter into the dough, flatten it to a 2-cm thick square under a sheet of baking parchment or cling film, using a rolling pin.

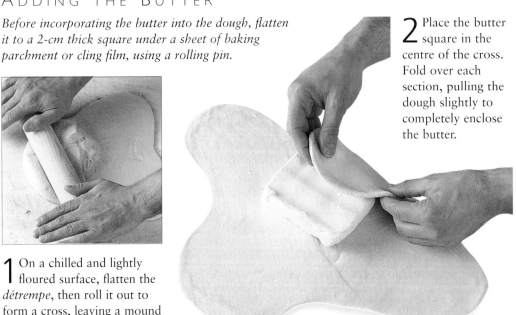

2 Place the butter square in the centre of the cross. Fold over each section, pulling the dough slightly to completely enclose the butter.

1 On a chilled and lightly floured surface, flatten the *détrempe*, then roll it out to form a cross, leaving a mound in the centre.

3 Lightly flour the work surface and roll over the top of the dough to seal the edges, then roll the dough into a rectangle.

ROLLING AND FOLDING THE DOUGH

In this stage, the dough is rolled out, then folded like a letter. It is important to keep the edges even and straight. Roll dough away from you with firm, even strokes.

1 Roll the dough into a 20- x 45-cm rectangle. Fold the bottom-third up towards the middle.

2 Bring the top-third of the dough over the folded thirds, and brush off any excess flour.

3 The dough should be square, have three layers and the edges should align. It now needs turning.

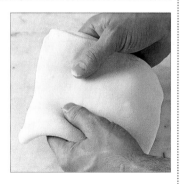

TURNING THE DOUGH

Puff pastry dough needs to be rolled, folded and turned a total of six times if it is to puff up and separate into layers. Mark the dough every "second" turn before chilling.

1 Give the square a quarter turn so that the exposed edge is on your right, as if the dough were a book. Gently press the edges to seal.

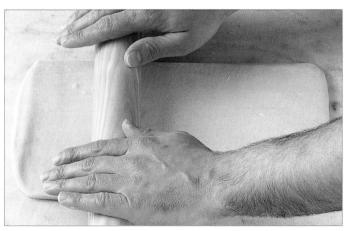

2 Roll out the dough into a 20- x 45-cm rectangle. Fold it again into thirds; seal edges. Chill for 30 minutes. Repeat rolling, folding and turning twice more.

MARKING THE DOUGH
Use your fingers to record how many turns you make.

QUICK TIPS FOR PUFF PASTRY

For best results, always work with puff pastry in a cool room and on a marble surface.

- Whenever possible, make puff pastry the day before it is to be used. This additional resting time makes the final dough easier to shape for baking.
- Perfect dough depends on the right proportion of ingredients. Some pastry chefs weigh the *détrempe* after mixing, then incorporate exactly half its weight in butter.
- Once the butter is wrapped in the *détrempe* package, chill it for an additional 30 minutes to bring them to the same temperature (this ensures a more even mixing).
- To ensure even rising, thorough chilling is essential after each second turn and the pastry should be scored before baking – this encourages the layers to rise evenly.
- As a further safeguard, chill the pastry one final time for 30 minutes after it has been cut into desired shape.
- Use an oven thermometer to ensure the pastry is baked at the proper temperature. If the oven is too cool, the butter in the dough will melt and the pastry will not rise properly.

SHAPING PUFF PASTRY

In classic French cuisine, puff pastry (see pages 16–17) is cut into shapes such as rectangles, rounds and diamonds and decoratively scored to make elegant crusts and airy, golden containers for sweet and savoury fillings.

MAKING BOUCHEES

These little cases are so-called because of their size – bouchée means mouthful. Bake on dampened baking sheets at 220°C, 20–25 minutes. To ensure straight rising, put a metal cutter at all four corners of the sheet and place another sheet on top. As bouchées rise, the top sheet prevents them toppling over.

1 Roll out two 3-mm thick sheets of dough. Lay one on top of the other; brush with egg wash (see page 43).

2 Chill or freeze pastry, then cut through both layers of dough with a 7.5-cm fluted pastry cutter.

3 Cut out the centres in the top layer of dough with an oiled 3.5-cm plain cutter.

MAKING A TRANCHE

Named after the French for slice, this decorative puff pastry case is used in classic French cuisine as a container for crème pâtissière and glazed fresh fruits, although other fillings can be used. Brush with egg wash (see page 43) and place on a dampened baking sheet before baking at 220°C for 8–12 minutes, then at 190°C for 12–15 minutes. Cool on a rack before filling.

1 Cut a 3-mm thick 14- x 30-cm rectangle. Trim edges neatly. Cut two 1-cm strips from the long edges.

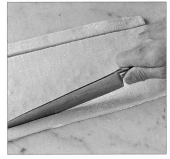

2 Brush long edges of rectangle with egg wash (see page 43). Place strips on top, 2 mm from edges. Score with the back of a knife.

MAKING FEUILLETES

These diamond-shaped pastries make stunning containers for creamy fillings and fresh fruits. Bake on dampened baking sheets at 220°C for 8–12 minutes, then at 190°C for 12–15 minutes. Cool on a rack before filling.

1 Roll out dough 3 mm thick. Cut into 13-cm squares. Fold each square in half diagonally to form a triangle.

2 Starting 1 cm in at the folded side, cut a 1-cm wide border along the open sides. Leave 1 cm uncut at end so strips remain attached.

3 Unfold the triangle and brush the edges of the inner square with egg wash (see page 43). Lift border strips and slip one strip under the other. Pull across the base to the opposite corners, then attach the points of the strips to the corners of the base with egg wash.

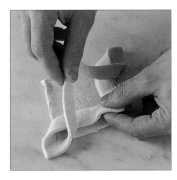

SWEET SAUCES

Sweet sauces give sweet pastries a decadent dimension. The technique for silky sabayon sauce, used both as a sauce and in classic French desserts, is an absolute must to learn. Crème Chantilly makes the ideal accompaniment for apple strudel and as a filling for whisked sponges.

MAKING A SABAYON SAUCE

This classic French sauce is a version of the Italian zabaglione. *It is not difficult to make, but care must be taken not to overheat the mixture or it may separate. It is usually served warm, but if you prefer it cold, remove it from the heat and whisk it constantly until it is cold.*

1 Whisk 6 egg yolks and 90 g caster sugar in a heatproof bowl until foamy and pale. Set bowl over a pan of simmering water.

2 Whisk constantly, adding 150 ml white dessert wine or fruit juice a little at a time, until the mixture begins to thicken.

3 Continue whisking until the mixture is thick enough to leave a ribbon trail. Finally, add 1 tbsp Madeira or sherry.

USES FOR SABAYON

Light and delicate, yet full of body, sabayon can be used as a base for parfaits, mousses and buttercream icing, but it is more often used as a sauce.

- Pour over fresh soft fruits, especially berries, and grill until caramelized.
- Serve as an accompaniment to warm fruit compotes and poached fruits.
- Serve with warm fruit tarts and pastries.
- Spoon around individual steamed puddings to make a pool of sauce.

MAKING SWEET SAUCES

These few basic sweet sauces yield surprisingly diverse and sumptuous textures. Brandy butter is melted over hot desserts, butterscotch sauce acts a tawny drizzle, and ethereal crème Chantilly is firm enough to pipe.

BRANDY BUTTER
Cream 175 g softened unsalted butter with a little icing sugar until light and soft. Add 4 tbsp brandy; beat until smooth. Chill.

BUTTERSCOTCH SAUCE
Stir 85 g butter, 175 g brown sugar and 2 tbsp golden syrup over a low heat until melted. Add 85 ml double cream and bring just to the boil.

CREME CHANTILLY
Whip 250 ml double cream until thickened. Add 2 tbsp caster sugar and a few drops of vanilla essence and whip until stiff peaks form.

Brandy Butter;
Butterscotch Sauce;
Crème Chantilly

CAKE MAKING

A perfectly baked cake requires more than just a good recipe and skilled mixing. It is vital to use the correct tins and to prepare them correctly. It is also essential to know how to tell just when a cake is fully baked.

BEST INGREDIENTS FOR CAKES

EGGS: Use fresh, medium-sized eggs. Take them from the refrigerator at least one hour before using – eggs at room temperature will incorporate more air and give a lighter result than eggs taken straight from the refrigerator.

FAT: Use unsalted butter, unless otherwise stated in recipe. For creamed cakes made by the all-in-one method (see page 22), use soft-tub margarine.

FLOUR: Most recipes specify plain flour plus an added raising agent such as baking powder or bicarbonate of soda. Self-raising flour includes its own raising agent and should only be used in recipes specifically calling for it.

SUGAR: For most recipes, use fine sugars such as caster or soft brown, both of which cream easily. Granulated sugar is not generally used, except for cakes made by the rubbing-in method.

GREASING AND FLOURING A CAKE TIN

For simple creamed cakes, such as Victoria sandwich, tea breads and fruit loaves, greasing and flouring is sufficient to prevent the batter sticking to the tin during baking and for the cake to turn out easily. Use melted unsalted butter, unless your recipe states otherwise.

1 Brush an even, thin layer of melted butter over the bottom, into the corners and up the sides of the cake tin.

2 Sprinkle with plain flour and rotate to coat evenly. Turn tin upside-down and tap centre to remove excess.

LINING A TIN

Some cakes, especially whisked sponges that have a tendency to stick, benefit from having a paper lining between them and the tin. For cakes such as sachertorte (see page 31), where a clean edge is important for perfect presentation, lining is vital. Non-stick baking parchment gives best results. Use the same technique for round, square and Swiss roll tins.

1 Stand tin on a sheet of baking parchment; draw around base with a pencil. Cut just inside the pencil line.

2 Grease the inside of the tin (see step 1, above), then place the baking parchment in the bottom.

DOUBLE LINING A DEEP TIN

Some rich fruit cakes have very long baking times, so to protect them from the oven's heat use a double lining. This will prevent the fruit burning and the crust overcooking. Once double lined, place a base liner (see above) into the tin. For extra protection, tie a folded newspaper around the outside of the tin.

1 Fold baking parchment sheet lengthwise in half. Wrap around tin. Mark 2 cm longer than circumference.

2 Snip 2-cm diagonal cuts along the folded edge, 3 cm apart. Secure inside tin, cut-edge down to line base.

3 Fold another baking parchment sheet in half, lengthwise. Wrap around tin and secure with tape.

LINING A LOAF TIN

Use the method shown here for lining a deep or shallow rectangular loaf tin. The cut corners of the lining paper will overlap in the tin, so use greaseproof paper, which is thinner then baking parchment, to reduce the bulk. Cut the paper to twice the size of the tin and centre the tin on the paper with the long sides of the tin parallel to the long sides of the paper.

1 Place tin in centre of the greaseproof paper. Make a diagonal cut from each corner to the corners of the tin.

2 Place the greaseproof paper inside tin and overlap the corners. Press into the corners and sides of tin.

TESTING FOR DONENESS

The cake should be golden and risen and shrinking slightly from the sides of the tin. There are two further tests, depending on the cake you are baking.

SPONGE CAKE
Lightly press the centre of the cake with your fingertips: it should spring back.

FRUIT CAKE
Insert a metal skewer in the centre of the cake: it should come out clean.

ADDING BATTER BEFORE BAKING

Soft light batters, such as creamed mixtures and whisked sponges, should be poured or spooned into tins, filling them half to two-thirds full. Heavy or dense batters, such as those for rich fruit cakes, need to be spooned in, filling the tin three-quarters full. Once the batter is in the tin, gently smooth the surface level to encourage even rising.

FRUIT CAKE BATTER
To prevent peaking and cracking, make a dip in centre with back of metal spoon.

SPONGE CAKE BATTER
Swirl with back of metal spoon. Mixture will find its own level during baking

TURNING OUT AND COOLING

After baking, let cakes stand in their tins for a while before turning out – sponge cakes need about 5 minutes standing, fruit cakes 30 minutes. Cooling on a wire rack ensures the bottom of the cake dries out and does not steam in its own heat.

1 Run a knife between the cake and the tin. Use one even movement. Short strokes could damage the cake crust.

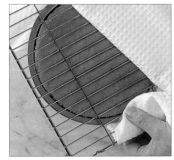

2 Place wire rack on top of cake. Hold with tea towel and invert the rack and tin so cake falls out on to rack.

3 Carefully peel off lining paper. Turn cake over and let cool on rack.

BASIC CAKES

The texture of a cake relies on both the ratio of its ingredients (varying amounts of fat, sugar, flour and eggs) and the method in which they are mixed. The techniques shown here produce three cakes of different densities and richness, all of which are easy to make.

VICTORIA SANDWICH

225 g self-raising flour
Pinch of salt
225 g butter, softened
225 g caster sugar
4 eggs
4 tbsp strawberry jam

Grease and flour two 20-cm round cake tins (see page 20). Sift the flour and salt together. Put the butter and sugar in a large bowl and cream together. In another bowl, lightly beat the eggs, then add them gradually to the creamed mixture. Gently fold in the flour. Spoon mixture into the prepared tins and bake at 190°C for 25 minutes. Turn out and let cool on a rack, then sandwich the cakes together with jam and dust cake top with caster sugar. Serves 6–8.

FLAVOURINGS FOR VICTORIA SANDWICH

Any of these can be added to the batter. For dry ingredients, replace a little of the flour; in the case of liquids, add them drop by drop.

- Grated citrus zest.
- Cocoa powder.
- Instant coffee granules dissolved in a little water.
- Vanilla or almond essence.
- Orange-flower water.
- Liqueurs, such as Cointreau.

THE CREAMING METHOD

The aim of using this technique is to incorporate as much air as possible. When mixing by hand, this is achieved by creaming the butter and sugar until almost white in colour, beating in the eggs slowly, then folding in the flour gently. For the all-in-one method shown in the tabletop mixer below, soft-tub margarine is needed to lighten the batter, plus baking powder to lift it.

BY HAND

1 Beat the butter and sugar together using a wooden spoon until the mixture is very light and fluffy.

2 Add eggs a little at a time, beating well after each addition. If mixture starts to curdle, add 1–2 tbsp flour.

3 Fold in the flour with a large metal spoon. Use a figure-of-eight movement to avoid knocking out air.

BY MACHINE

1 Put ingredients in a table-top mixer, using soft-tub margarine instead of butter. Add 1½ tsp baking powder.

2 Beat together on medium speed until the batter is creamy, smooth and well blended, 2–3 minutes.

TRICK OF THE TRADE

MAKING A LIGHTER BATTER

Fold 1–2 tbsp warm water into the batter immediately before spooning it into the cake tin.

THE RUBBING-IN METHOD

The essential technique here is to rub the fat into the flour until evenly distributed – stop rubbing when the mixture resembles fine breadcrumbs.

1 Rub the butter into the flour between your fingers and thumbs. Lift your hands up out of the bowl as you rub. This will incorporate air into the mixture.

2 Add the sugar and mixed dried fruits and stir until all of the ingredients are evenly mixed.

3 After adding the egg and milk, incorporate the flour from the sides gradually and mix together well.

TRICK OF THE TRADE

PREVENTING FRUITS SINKING

Dried fruits are heavy and tend to sink to the bottom of cake batters; this simple but clever technique helps combat the problem.

Toss the fruits in a little of the measured flour before starting to make the batter. The flour creates a dry coating around the fruits which helps to suspend them within the cake mixture and prevent them absorbing too much of the liquid.

MIXED FRUIT CAKE

450 g plain flour
1 tsp ground mixed spice
1 tsp ground ginger
1 tsp bicarbonate of soda
225 g mixed dried fruits
175 g butter, softened
225 g brown sugar
1 egg, beaten
About 300 ml milk

Grease and line a deep 23-cm round cake tin (see page 20). Sift the flour, ground spices and bicarbonate of soda into a bowl. Remove 2 tbsp and mix this with the fruits (see box, left).

Rub the butter into the flour to resemble fine breadcrumbs. Stir in the sugar and dried fruits.

Make a well in the centre, add the egg and milk and mix to a soft dropping consistency, adding a little more milk if necessary. Spoon into the prepared tin and level the surface. Bake at 170°C for about 1 hour 40 minutes. Turn the cake out and let cool on a rack. Serves 10–12.

THE MELTING METHOD

This is one of the simplest of cake-making techniques, relying on a melted mixture of butter, sugar and treacle for moistness and bicarbonate of soda for lightness. Measure the treacle accurately – too much will result in a heavy cake. The bicarbonate of soda will begin to work as soon as the ingredients are mixed, so work quickly.

1 Stir butter, sugar and treacle over a low heat with a wooden spoon until just melted. Let cool slightly.

2 Pour slightly cooled melted mixture into egg and milk, mix well, then start to stir in flour from sides.

3 Beat with a wooden spoon until the mixture is smooth, with a dropping consistency.

GINGERBREAD

250 g each butter, dark
brown sugar and black treacle
375 g plain flour
1 tbsp ground ginger
1 tsp each ground mixed spice
and nutmeg
2 tsp bicarbonate of soda
1 egg, beaten
300 ml milk

Grease and line a 23-cm square cake tin (see page 20). Melt butter, sugar and treacle. Cool slightly. Sift dry ingredients into a bowl, add egg, milk and melted mixture and beat well. Pour into prepared tin. Bake at 170°C for about 1½ hours. Turn out and let cool on a rack. Serves 10–12.

WHISKED CAKES

A whisked sponge boasts the lightest texture of all cakes. Its volume relies on the amount of air incorporated when eggs are whisked with sugar over a gentle heat. Butter can be included for richness.

BASIC WHISKED SPONGE CAKE

4 eggs
120 g caster sugar
120 g plain flour, sifted with
  a pinch of salt

Grease, flour and line a 20-cm round cake tin (see page 20). Whisk the eggs and sugar in a heatproof bowl over a pan of hot water until the mixture is thick. Remove the bowl from the pan of hot water and continue whisking off the heat until the mixture is cool. Sift and fold in the flour. Pour into the prepared tin and bake at 170°C for about 25 minutes. Turn out, remove paper and let cool on a wire rack. Serves 6–8.

SERVING A WHISKED SPONGE

A plain whisked sponge can be simply layered with whipped cream and jam and sprinkled with caster or icing sugar, or it can be elaborately decorated. Try one of the following ideas.

- Fill with raspberry mousse and whole raspberries (as shown in the Swiss roll, opposite page).
- Imbibe with sugar syrup and liqueur, then layer and coat with whipped cream and fruit purée (see page 27).
- Fill and decorate with crème Chantilly and fresh fruits (see page 33).

MAKING A WHISKED SPONGE

Pastry chefs use a very large balloon whisk to incorporate as much air as possible, but you can use a hand-held electric whisk if you prefer. To speed up the thickening process, the bowl is set over hot water – take care not to let it touch the water or the mixture will start to cook.

1 Put the eggs and sugar in large heatproof bowl and whisk vigorously for a few seconds to break up the eggs and start mixing them with the sugar.

2 Put the bowl over a pan of hot water and whisk until the mixture is thick enough to leave a figure-of-eight ribbon trail on the surface when the whisk is lifted.

3 Remove the bowl from the heat and continue whisking until the mixture has cooled and is very thick, 3–5 minutes.

4 Fold in flour in batches with a rubber spatula. Cut cleanly through, to avoid knocking out the air.

5 Pour finished batter slowly into the prepared tin, gently guiding it in with the spatula.

6 When fully cooked, the sponge will be golden, well risen and firm but springy to the touch.

ENRICHING A WHISKED SPONGE

Add melted butter to the basic whisked sponge mixture to enrich the batter and make it more moist. Take care that the butter is thoroughly cooled after melting and add it to the whisked mixture slowly, after the flour has been folded in. Bake the cake as soon as possible after mixing or batter may deflate.

1 Melt 20 g unsalted butter and let cool. Pour slowly over the surface of the whisked mixture.

2 Gently fold in the butter, cutting through the mixture with a spatula so as not to knock air out of it, until evenly incorporated.

WHAT'S IN A NAME?

A whisked sponge is often called a Genoese sponge cake or *génoise* in French. Considered one of the great French classics in cake making, it actually originated in Genoa, northern Italy, hence its name. Recipes vary – some are fatless, while others enriched with melted butter. For layered cakes, the fatless sponge is lighter – butter gives a denser texture.

MAKING A SWISS ROLL

The sponge for a Swiss roll is baked in a shallow rectangular tin, then turned out, cooled and rolled around a filling. Follow the whisked sponge technique on the opposite page, using 4 eggs, 125 g sugar and 75 g plain flour. Bake in a 22- x 33-cm Swiss roll tin at 190-200°C, 4–5 minutes. For fillings, see box, opposite page.

1 Lift sponge out of tin on lining paper and place on wire rack. Let cool.

2 Place crust-side down on parchment dusted with sugar. Peel off lining paper.

4 Carefully roll up the sponge, using the baking parchment to help. For a tighter roll, see box, right. Place finished Swiss roll, seam-side down, and dust with icing or caster sugar just before serving.

TRICK OF THE TRADE

Use this chef's technique to tighten a Swiss roll for a neat presentation.

Push a palette knife under the sponge in the parchment. Pull the parchment away from the knife.

3 Transfer sponge, still on the baking parchment, to a tea towel. Spread over your chosen filling. Fold over 2 cm of sponge along one long edge, using the parchment to guide you. This will make rolling easier.

SPECIAL CAKES

These cakes rely on special techniques involving the ingredients used, and the way the cakes are made and assembled. Added interest and flavour are achieved pastry-chef style by imbibing layers and stacking them.

12 egg whites (about 350 ml)

1 1/2 tsp cream of tartar

280 g caster sugar

85 g plain flour, sifted

25 g cornflour, sifted

1 tsp vanilla essence

Whisk the egg whites until foaming, then add the cream of tartar and continue whisking until stiff. Add the sugar, 1 tbsp at a time, whisking after each addition to form a stiff meringue. Fold in the flour, cornflour and vanilla. Pour into an ungreased angel cake or tube tin and bake at 175°C for 40–45 minutes. Invert tin and leave cake to cool in the tin. Serves 10–12.

MAKING AN ANGEL FOOD CAKE

This famous American cake is unusual in that it is made with just egg whites, no yolks, which is why it is so light and airy. Cream of tartar is whisked with the whites to stiffen them and give the meringue body, and the cake is cooled upside down in the tin to prevent shrinkage and preserve the shape.

1 Fold flour, cornflour and vanilla into meringue with a spatula until just blended. Do not overmix or air will be knocked out.

2 Pour batter into an ungreased and unfloured angel cake tin. Level the surface with the spatula and bake immediately.

3 After baking, invert cake in tin on to its feet. If tin has no feet, invert tin on to a funnel or bottle neck. Cool completely, then unmould.

225 g unsalted butter, softened

150 g soft brown sugar

4 eggs, separated

200 g chilled unsweetened chocolate, grated

200 g ground hazelnuts

25 g ground almonds

50 g caster sugar

Grease and line a 23-cm round cake tin (see page 20). Cream butter and sugar, then beat in egg yolks. Add grated chocolate and ground nuts and beat well to mix. Whisk egg whites in a separate bowl until stiff, then whisk in sugar. Fold into chocolate mixture. Pour into tin and bake at 150°C, 50 minutes. Serves 10–12.

MAKING A CHOCOLATE TORTE

Austrian-style tortes have no flour, hence their rich, dense textures. In such flourless cakes, nuts replace the flour, ground very fine so they release some of their oil and give the cake a close crumb. Good-quality chocolate with a high cocoa butter content is absolutely essential.

1 Beat grated chocolate and ground nuts into creamed ingredients until they are evenly mixed.

2 Fold the meringue very carefully into the nut mixture, in 3–4 batches, using a spatula.

3 Press centre of baked cake with your finger: it should feel slightly soft. During cooling, texture will firm up.

CUTTING AND IMBIBING

For a layered cake to have a neat finish, the layers must be cut accurately. The technique used here ensures even layers that line up perfectly when the cake is reassembled (see right). Imbibing the layers with sugar syrup and liqueur is the professional way to give moistness and flavour.

1 Make a notch down the side of the cake with the blade of a small knife.

2 Cut cake into two or three layers, using a serrated knife and a sawing action.

3 Brush cut surfaces with a light sugar syrup and 2–3 tbsp liqueur.

FILLING AND LAYERING

After cutting and imbibing (see left), cake layers can be reassembled with the filling of your choice. Whipped cream and raspberry purée are shown here; for other filling ideas, see box, page 24. Save the base of the cake for the last, top layer because it has the flattest surface.

1 Spread filling over one cake layer. Top with next layer, lining up notches, and repeat.

2 Top with the last cake layer, cut-side down, again matching up notches.

3 Spread the top and sides of the cake with filling, using a warm palette knife.

MAKING A MERINGUE CAKE

Pastry chefs use this professional layering technique to create cakes with a very precise finish. Here meringue discs are layered with chocolate mousse, but you can use the same technique for the layers of sponge cake and cream filling shown above. For the technique of making the chocolate cigarettes for the decoration, see page 45.

1 Place a meringue disc on a cake card in a metal ring. Add a layer of mousse to cover it. Cover with another disc and continue the layers, finishing with mousse. Chill in the refrigerator until set.

2 Wrap a warm cloth around the metal ring for 1–2 minutes, then carefully lift the ring off the cake.

CHEESECAKES

Baked or unbaked, with biscuit crumb or pastry crust, ever-popular cheesecakes are very easy to make. The cake itself can be light and fluffy, or sumptuous and rich, depending on the method and type of cheese used.

RASPBERRY CHEESECAKE

250 g digestive biscuits, crushed
60 g butter, melted
15 g gelatine powder
4 tbsp water
125 ml double cream
500 ml unsweetened berry purée
125 g caster sugar
250 g curd cheese

Base-line a 25-cm springform tin with biscuits and butter and chill. Prepare the gelatine in the water. Whip the cream. Mix remaining ingredients, stir in dissolved gelatine, then fold in cream. Pour into tin. Chill at least 4 hours; unmould. Serves 6–8.

MAKING A CRUMB BASE

Biscuit crumb bases, held together by melted butter, are usually chilled in the refrigerator until set and used for refrigerator cheesecakes as here, but they can also be used for baked cheesecakes (see opposite page). If you like you can crush the biscuits in a food processor.

1 Break the biscuits into pieces. Place them in a heavy-duty plastic bag and crush them by tapping and rolling with a rolling pin.

2 Transfer the crushed biscuits to a large bowl, pour in the melted butter and stir with a metal spoon until they are evenly mixed.

3 Press the biscuit crust into the bottom of the tin with the back of the metal spoon, smoothing and flattening it so the layer is even.

MAKING A CHILLED CHEESECAKE

Fruit purée, curd cheese and whipped cream are set with gelatine to make a mousse-like texture that is firm enough to slice. This type of cheesecake, also called a refrigerator cheesecake, is lighter than the baked variety. A simple recipe using this technique is given above.

REMOVING SIDE OF TIN
Set tin over a bowl that is slightly smaller than the base; gently ease down the side of tin, leaving the cheesecake on the metal base.

ADDING GELATINE
Stir cooled, dissolved gelatine into berry purée and cheese mixture until evenly mixed, using a spatula.

RELEASING CLIP
Slowly release the spring on the side of the tin; this will loosen the edge and free the cheesecake.

MAKING A BAKED CHEESECAKE

This type of cheesecake is traditionally baked in a pastry case. Here a crisp, sweet Austrian-style pastry that has been enriched with cream cheese is used, but you can use a plain pâte brisée or sweet pâte sucrée if you prefer. Pastry cases should always be baked blind first, to prevent the filling making them soggy.

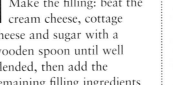

1 Make the filling: beat the cream cheese, cottage cheese and sugar with a wooden spoon until well blended, then add the remaining filling ingredients and stir together until the flour and the cornflour are evenly incorporated.

2 Line bottom of tin with a circle of pastry, then line side with a deep strip. Make sure all edges are sealed, to prevent the filling leaking out during baking.

3 After removing foil and baking beans, ladle the cheese filling into the partially baked crust. It should come almost to the top of the pastry case.

4 When the cheesecake is cooked, the pastry case will have shrunk away from the side of the tin and a fine skewer inserted into the centre will come out clean.

AUSTRIAN CHEESECAKE

375 g cream cheese
350 g cottage cheese
175 g caster sugar
4 eggs, lightly beaten
125 ml sour cream
215 g plain flour
1 tbsp cornflour
2–3 tbsp water

Make the filling: beat 250 g cream cheese with the cottage cheese and 100 g sugar. Stir in the eggs, sour cream, 2 tbsp of the flour and the cornflour.

Make the pastry: rub the remaining cream cheese into the remaining flour. Stir in the remaining sugar and enough water to bind the dough. Chill for 30 minutes. Roll out and line the base and sides of a 25-cm springform tin. Bake blind at 180°C for 10–15 minutes. Pour in filling and bake for 45–50 minutes until set. Cool in the tin, then unmould. Serves 12.

5 To decorate, place a paper doily on top of cake. Put icing sugar in a small fine sieve and shake gently over top of cheesecake. Carefully remove the doily. Alternatively, cover top of cheesecake with glazed berries or chocolate curls (see page 44).

CAKE ICING

Even the plainest of cakes can be transformed into a real treat with the addition of icing – either simply swirled or skilfully piped. Glacé, royal, chocolate and buttercream are the easy-to-master basics, while the art of whipped crème Chantilly is one of the pastry chef's best-kept secrets.

MAKING A PAPER PIPING BAG

Use baking parchment. The tip of the bag can be cut to vary its size.

Cut a 25-cm square of paper in half diagonally. Bring one point of triangle to centre to form cone.

Wrap the remaining point of the triangle around to meet the other two points.

Pull all 3 points tightly together to create a sharp tip and fold flap inside; crease to hold the shape.

MAKING GLACE ICING

This simple icing is traditionally made with icing sugar and warm water, but many pastry chefs like to cut its sweetness by using fruit juice or a liqueur instead. To coat the top and sides of a 20-cm cake, use 175 g icing sugar and 1–2 tbsp liquid. Use the icing immediately after making.

1 Sift icing sugar into a bowl. Work hard lumps through with a metal spoon.

2 Add a little warm water or flavouring of your choice and whisk vigorously.

3 Continue whisking until smooth, adding more liquid as necessary.

MAKING ROYAL ICING

To delay setting and make icing easy to work with, the trick of the trade is to add glycerine. For the top and sides of a 24-cm cake, use 500 g icing sugar, 2 egg whites, 2 tbsp lemon juice and 2 tsp glycerine. Cover icing with cling film, let stand overnight and stir before using.

1 Put sifted icing sugar in a bowl and make a well in the centre. Add lightly beaten egg whites and lemon juice.

2 Whisk until stiff and glossy, about 10 minutes, then whisk in glycerine.

MAKING CHOCOLATE ICING

A glossy professional-looking icing, as on the sachertorte below, is easy to make following the technique here. Good-quality unsweetened chocolate is essential – here couverture buttons (pistoles) are used for ease of melting. Glaze the cake (see box, below) before making the icing.

1 Add chocolate to sugar syrup, then whisk over a moderate heat until well combined and smooth.

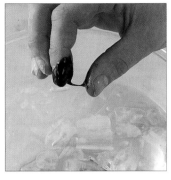

2 To test for the thread stage, dip fingers in iced water, then into chocolate. Pull apart to see thread.

3 Stand pan on tea towel and tap lightly to knock out any air bubbles. Use immediately (see below).

CHOCOLATE ICING

150 g caster sugar
150 ml water
300 g chocolate pistoles

Make a sugar syrup with the sugar and water. Add the chocolate pieces and whisk until combined. Cook over a low heat for 3–5 minutes until just before the soft-ball stage, when the "thread" stage is reached (110°C). Remove pan from heat and tap on the work surface to eliminate air bubbles. Use immediately. Makes enough icing to coat a 25-cm cake.

TRICK OF THE TRADE

MAKING A GLAZE

Jam glazes are used to coat cakes before icing to give a smooth finish and add moisture; they are also used over fruits in tarts and tartlets to keep them fresh and give sparkle.

Melt 100 g jam (use apricot for chocolate cakes; red fruit jam for fruits). Work warm jam through a sieve to remove lumps of fruit. Return to pan, add 50 ml water and bring to the boil, stirring. To glaze cake, place on a rack and brush warm glaze all over.

COATING WITH CHOCOLATE ICING

For a flawless finish, work quickly, and with a steady hand. Before the cake is iced, place it on a wire rack over baking parchment to catch the drips and prevent the icing from pooling around the bottom of the cake. After it has set, the icing will be glossy and smooth.

1 Ladle warm chocolate icing (see above) over the centre of cake coated with apricot-jam glaze (see left).

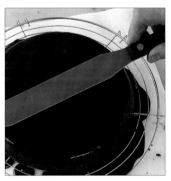

2 Quickly smooth icing across top of cake with a warm palette knife. Allow excess to run down sides.

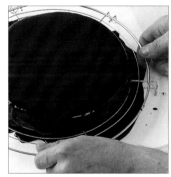

3 Tap rack on work surface so icing settles. Leave to set, about 5–10 minutes.

FINISHING

Melted chocolate is easy to pipe from a paper piping bag and it looks very effective. A classic example of this is shown on the Austrian sachertorte, *simply but elegantly decorated with its name.*

Fill a paper piping bag (see opposite page) with melted chocolate. Fold over the top to seal, then trim the tip. Squeeze the chocolate out of the bag as you write the name.

BUTTERCREAM ICING

160 g caster sugar

85 ml water

2 egg yolks

1 egg

250 g unsalted butter, softened

Make a sugar syrup with the sugar and water and heat to the soft-ball stage. Lightly beat the egg yolks and egg in a tabletop mixer fitted with the whisk attachment. With the motor running, pour a thin, steady stream of sugar syrup down the side of the bowl. Whisk until the mixture is mousse-like, pale in colour and cool. Cut butter into chunks and gradually add to the bowl. Increase to full speed and whisk for 3–4 minutes until butter is incorporated. When pale and fluffy, add flavouring if you like. Makes enough icing to coat a 24-cm cake.

MAKING BUTTERCREAM ICING

This ultrasmooth rich frosting is made by whisking butter into a sabayon of eggs and sugar syrup. The sabayon should be at cool room temperature before adding the butter – too hot and the butter will melt, too cold and it will set. Buttercream can be used as a cake filling or coating, plain or flavoured with vanilla or coffee essence, or with a liqueur or praline paste.

1 Boil the sugar syrup to the soft-ball stage. To test without a thermometer, dip your fingers in iced water, then quickly into the syrup – the syrup that sticks to your fingers should hold its shape but feel soft when pressed.

2 Whisking on medium speed, pour the hot sugar syrup in a thin steady stream down the side of the mixer bowl into the egg yolks and egg. Continue whisking on medium speed to make a sabayon (see page 19) that is pale, thick and cool.

3 With the machine whisking on full speed, add chunks of softened butter to the mixture, making sure that each piece is completely blended in before adding the next. When the butter is incorporated, whisk in the flavouring of your choice.

MAKING BUTTERCREAM

This simple frosting is most often used for children's birthday cakes and novelty cakes. Made as a simple alternative to the professional buttercream above, it is particularly favoured because it requires no special skill or equipment.

Cream 125 g unsalted butter with a wooden spoon until soft. Gradually beat in 250 g sifted icing sugar until the mixture is smooth and pale, then add a few drops of flavouring or colouring if you like. Continue beating until the mixture is very pale and fluffy, adding a little warm water if the icing is too stiff.

4 Lift whisk out of bowl and scrape off buttercream. Refrigerate for 5–10 minutes to firm up the butter in the mixture. The buttercream is now ready to use.

ICING WITH CREAM

One of the quickest, easiest and most effective ways to fill and ice a cake is with whipped cream. Pastry chefs frequently use crème Chantilly (see page 19) – its vanilla flavour goes well with plain sponge cake and fresh fruits to make a truly fabulous dessert. Here a whisked sponge cake (see page 24) is used, cut into three layers and imbibed with sugar syrup and kirsch. For a 25-cm cake, you will need about 500 ml cream and 200 g fruit.

1 Cut and imbibe the cake (see page 27); place on a cake card. Spread the layers with crème Chantilly and top with thinly sliced fresh fruits, arranging them in even layers.

2 Smooth any excess filling around the sides of the cake with a palette knife, then spread an even layer of crème Chantilly over the top of the cake, making the surface as smooth as possible.

3 Using a "paddling" motion with the tip of the palette knife, spread more cream on the sides, rotating the cake with the help of a turntable if available.

4 Use a flat scraper to smooth off the sides. Keep it at a 45° angle as you rotate the cake. Repeat with a toothed scraper to make a decorative ridged edge.

5 Transfer cake to a smaller card. Place the cake on an icing turntable over a sheet of paper; gently press chopped toasted nuts around the base.

6 Score the top of the cake into twelve equal sections with the tip of a sharp knife, then pipe a rosette of cream on each section using a large star nozzle.

7 Decorate the top of the cake as shown, with strawberry halves dipped in red jam glaze (see box, page 31) and nuts. Alternatively, experiment with fruits, nuts, and flavourings of your choice.

TRICK OF THE TRADE
●

SOFTENING JAM
Pastry chefs use this technique to prevent jam from tearing cakes when it is spread over layers.

Put seedless or sieved jam on the work surface or a clean, smooth board and work it back and forth with a palette knife until it has a very soft, spreading consistency. This technique is especially useful for whisked sponge cakes made without fat, because they have a delicate crumb. The thin layer of cake in a Swiss roll (see page 25) is particularly delicate and may break up if spread with unsoftened jam.

PETITS FOURS

Dainty, demure and splendidly frivolous, these playful bites are the debutantes of desserts. Petit fours – a range of delicate and exquisite cakes, biscuits, fruits and chocolate – demand close attention to detail; even the simplified versions. Bake with care; they scorch easily.

LACE TUILES

70 ml orange juice
Grated zest of 1 orange
50 ml Grand Marnier
250 g caster sugar
100 g unsalted butter, melted
200 g nibbed almonds
125 g plain flour

Mix all the ingredients in a bowl. Butter a baking sheet and place small spoonfuls of mixture on to the sheet, five at a time. Flatten each one with a fork and bake at 180°C, 5 minutes. Remove the tuiles and place on oiled rolling pins to set shapes as you make the next five. Makes 25.

FINANCIERS

30 g raisins
3 tbsp rum
60 g unsalted butter, melted
60 g egg whites
60 g caster sugar
30 g plain flour
30 g ground almonds

Butter six small oval tartlet moulds and chill. Soak the raisins in rum for at least 15 minutes. Mix all the ingredients together until smooth. Add raisins. Divide one-quarter of the mixture between the moulds and bake at 200°C, 10 minutes. Remove from oven and repeat three times with the remaining mixture. Imbibe with remaining rum. Makes 24.

LACE TUILES
Tuile is the French word for roof tile and these delicious delicacies are so-called because of their shape.

OPERETTAS
Make a Swiss roll sponge (see page 25) and cut cake into three. Spread one piece with ganache. Cover with another piece and imbibe with a coffee-flavoured sugar syrup. Spread sponge with buttercream icing (see page 32) and top with the remaining sponge. Coat with chocolate fondant and let set. Cut into squares and top each one with gold leaf. Makes 21.

FINANCIERS
These are small sponge cakes which can be flavoured in a variety of ways. Try replacing rum with *eau de vie* or substitute nuts or other dried fruits for the raisins.

CARAMEL-COATED PHYSALIS
Gently peel back the leaves of physalis and twist at the base. Make a light caramel syrup. Dip each berry into the caramel, leaving the leaves uncoated, and allow any excess to drip off. Place upright on greased baking parchment and allow to set.

ICE-CREAM BALLS

Use a melon baller to shape ice cream into small balls. Working quickly to keep ice cream solid, place balls on baking parchment and insert a cocktail stick in each one. Freeze balls for 10 minutes. Dip ice-cream balls into cooled melted chocolate until balls are evenly coated, then place at an angle on baking parchment and leave to set.

CITRON TARTLETS

Make half the pâte sucrée (see page 6). Line 6 tiny tartlet moulds with pastry and bake at 180°C, about 7–10 minutes. Unmould and repeat five times. Make half the crème patissière (see page 39) and add the juice of 2 lemons. Pour custard into each tart and sprinkle with icing sugar. Caramelize tops with a blow torch. Makes 30.

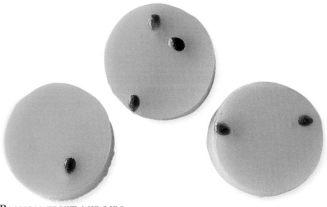

PASSION FRUIT MIROIRS

ALMOND TRUFFLES

1 Make a fruit mousse with passion fruit and set in a tin. Coat with a fruit jelly. Chill until set.

2 Cut out miroirs using 4-cm metal cutters. Place miroirs on baking parchment and chill in the refrigerator until serving time.

1 Shape almond paste into small balls with a melon baller and dip into ganache made with white chocolate until coated.

2 Roll each truffle over a wire cooling rack to create a spiked effect. Leave truffles on rack to set, then place in petit-four cases.

BISCUITS

From simple rolled, sliced and piped biscuits based on similar doughs, to buttery shortbread, crisp brandy snaps and classic French sponge fingers and *tuiles*, biscuits appear in a seemingly endless array of shapes, textures and flavours. The following techniques reveal some of the best.

BASIC DOUGHS

ROLLED BISCUITS: Soften 125 g unsalted butter and cream with 150 g caster sugar. When smooth, beat in 2 egg yolks and 225 g plain flour. Add 50 g raisins, currants or sultanas. Shape biscuits; bake at 180°C, 15 minutes. Makes 12–15.

DROPPED BISCUITS: Melt 125 g unsalted butter. Add 150 g caster sugar. When cool, mix in 2 egg whites, then 100 g plain flour and 125 g ground almonds. Shape biscuits, then bake at 180°C, 15 minutes. Makes 12–15.

SHORTBREAD

115 g butter, softened
55 g caster sugar
115 g plain flour

Cream the butter and sugar until light and fluffy. Stir in the flour. Spoon the mixture into a buttered 31- x 21-cm tin and press down with your fingertips to compress and level the dough.

Mark the dough into bars of equal size, without cutting through to the base of the tin. Bake at 170°C for 35 minutes or until shortbread is pale golden brown. Cool in the tin for about 5 minutes, then sprinkle with sugar and cut into bars. Let cool in the tin for about 1 hour, then lift out and cool completely on a wire rack. Makes 18 bars.

ROLLED BISCUITS

For these biscuits, the dough (see box, left) is firm enough to roll and cut out, or roll and slice. It spreads very little on the baking sheet during cooking, so there is no need to space the shapes very far apart. Lightly knead the dough until it just comes together, then chill. Re-roll trimmings only once – any more than this and the biscuits will be tough.

ROLLING AND CUTTING
Chill dough, then roll out. Cut out shapes using a floured biscuit cutter.

ROLLING AND SLICING
Roll dough into a log, then wrap and chill in the refrigerator until firm. Cut the dough log crosswise into even slices with a knife.

MAKING SHORTBREAD

This shortbread is made with ground rice, which gives it a crisp texture, but you can use semolina instead. If you like, shape the mixture in a round on a baking sheet, either freeform or, more precisely, inside a metal ring. Round shortbreads traditionally have crimped edges.

1 Press dough firmly into buttered tin with your fingertips, making sure that it is even in thickness.

2 While still warm, sprinkle shortbread with caster sugar, then cut into bars with a large chef's knife.

3 After cooling shortbread in tin for 5 minutes, transfer bars to a rack and let cool completely.

DROPPED BISCUITS

These biscuits are made with a slacker dough than the rolled biscuits (see box, opposite page), soft enough to be dropped from a spoon or piped on to a baking sheet, without needing to be rolled out first. Make sure the shapes are the same size to ensure even baking, and space them well apart as the dough tends to spread.

FREE-FORM
Place mounds or drop teaspoonfuls of the dough on to the baking sheet.

PIPED
Fill a piping bag fitted with a star nozzle with dough. Pipe rosettes on to baking sheet.

FINISHING

To enhance the appearance, flavour and texture of biscuits, try the following.

SPRINKLING SUGAR
For a crunchy texture, sprinkle demerara sugar on to shapes before baking. For extra crunch, add more sugar after baking, if you like.

CHOCOLATE COVERING
Spread melted chocolate over one side of biscuits after baking, then mark with a fork if you like. Let set, chocolate-side up, on a rack.

BRANDY SNAPS

These light, lacy-textured biscuits are shaped after baking, while they are still warm and malleable. If you work quickly they should not harden, but if they do, pop them back in the oven to soften for about 30 seconds.

1 Space teaspoonfuls of batter well apart on baking sheet; press each one with your fingertips to spread it out to a 3-cm round.

2 Let the biscuits rest for one minute after baking, then lift off the baking sheet with a palette knife.

3 Curl each brandy snap, lacy-side out around the greased spoon, overlapping the edges slightly. Slip off and cool on a wire rack.

BRANDY SNAPS

115 g butter
115 g demerara sugar
2 tbsp golden syrup
115 g plain flour
1 tsp ground ginger
1 tsp brandy

Melt butter, sugar and syrup. Stir in flour, ginger and brandy. Put four well-spaced teaspoonfuls of mixture on a greased baking sheet. Bake at 180°C for 7–10 minutes. Shape one at a time around a greased wooden spoon handle while still warm. Repeat five times. Makes 20.

SPONGE FINGERS

3 eggs, separated
100 g caster sugar
75 g plain flour, sifted
Icing sugar, for dusting

Grease a baking sheet and line with baking parchment. Whisk egg whites until soft peaks form, then gradually whisk in half the caster sugar until stiff and glossy. In a separate bowl, lightly beat egg yolks with the remaining caster sugar, then fold into the meringue followed by the flour. Pipe on to prepared baking sheet and dust with icing sugar in two batches. Bake at 180°C until golden brown, 10 minutes. Let cool on a wire rack. Makes 10–12.

STENCIL PASTE

3 egg whites
100 g icing sugar
100 g plain flour
60 g unsalted butter, melted
Vanilla essence (optional)

Whisk the egg whites and icing sugar together until smooth. Stir in the flour and whisk lightly until just combined. Pour in melted butter, and a few drops of vanilla essence if using, and stir gently until smooth. Cover and let rest in the refrigerator, 30 minutes. For *tuiles*, grease a baking sheet and a rolling pin. Place six teaspoonfuls of batter on baking sheet; spread into 5-cm circles with a wet fork. Bake at 200°C for 5–8 minutes until golden at the edges. Shape while warm on greased rolling pin; repeat with remaining mixture. Makes 18. For *tulipes*, bake as for *tuiles*, using tablespoonfuls of batter and spreading each one into a 10-cm circle. While warm, shape in two moulds. Makes 8–10.

MAKING SPONGE FINGERS

These light, airy sponge fingers are made by enriching a meringue mixture with egg yolks. Gently fold the ingredients together to prevent knocking out the air. The double dusting technique creates the characteristic "pearls" of sugar on top of the fingers.

1 Pipe batter fingers with a 2-cm plain nozzle on baking parchment. Make them 10 cm long and 5 cm apart.

2 Before baking, dust fingers with half the icing sugar. Let stand until sugar has dissolved, then dust again.

3 Holding the parchment in place, lift one side of the baking sheet and tip off the excess sugar.

MAKING TUILES

Pastry chefs use a classic French stencil paste (see box, left) to make these delicate, curved biscuits, named after the French word for roof tiles. Shape the mixture straight from the oven, while still soft.

SHAPING BATTER
Use the back of a fork dipped in cold water to prevent the batter sticking.

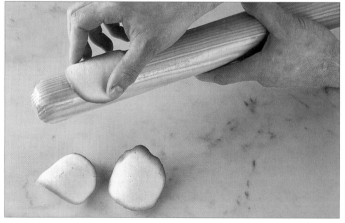

SHAPING BISCUITS
Immediately after baking, shape the biscuits around a greased rolling pin to form curved *tuiles*. Let cool on a wire rack.

MAKING TULIPES

These ruffled biscuits are made from the same stencil paste as tuiles *(see left), but they are shaped to make containers – for filling with fruits and ice creams.*

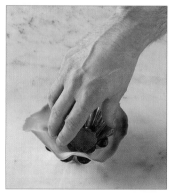

Immediately after baking, press each shape into a small fluted mould then, while the shape is still warm, gently press a smaller mould inside the first to form a tulip-shaped container. Carefully remove the moulds and place the *tulipe* on a wire rack until cold and firm.

CUSTARDS & CREAMS

The luxurious marriage of milk, sugar and eggs is the foundation for silky sauces, vanilla-scented creams and thick, smooth custards. The following methods make use of similar ingredients, but techniques, cooking times and added enrichments create different tastes and textures.

CREME ANGLAISE

Cooking an egg custard on the stove top requires close attention. So the eggs do not curdle, make sure the milk does not boil while the custard is cooking. Keep the heat gentle and stir constantly around the sides and bottom of the pan to prevent the possibility of scorching.

1 Infuse 500 ml milk with ½ vanilla pod. Whisk 5 egg yolks in a bowl with 65 g caster sugar. Remove vanilla pod from the milk and bring the milk to the boil. Whisk milk into eggs, then pour into a clean pan.

2 Heat the custard gently, stirring constantly with a wooden spoon, until it thickens. Test consistency by running your finger through the custard along the back of spoon. It should leave a clear line. Makes about 625 ml.

CREME PATISSIERE

If not using immediately, rub butter over the surface to prevent a skin forming.

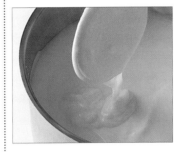

Whisk 6 egg yolks in a bowl with 100 g caster sugar, then whisk in 40 g each plain flour and cornflour. Bring 600 ml milk to the boil and stir into egg mixture. Pour into a pan and bring back to the boil, stirring until large bubbles break on surface. Lower the heat and cook until very thick.

BAKING CUSTARDS

English custards are baked in a large dish and served hot. Blend 3 egg yolks with 50 g sugar and 25 g each cornflour and plain flour. Add 500 ml milk and cook gently, stirring, until thickened, then pour into dish. In France, custards are baked in pretty little pots and served cold. The custard is the same as the English one, but made with 300 ml double cream and 200 ml milk, plus 2 egg yolks.

TRADITIONAL ENGLISH
Grate nutmeg over top of custard in baking dish and bake in a warm *bain marie* at 170°C for 20-25 minutes. Serve the custard hot.

FRENCH PETITS POTS
Bake individual pots of enriched custard in a cold *bain marie* at 170 °C for 15-20 minutes. Cool, then chill before serving.

WHAT'S IN A NAME?

CREME ANGLAISE: This is a rich custard sauce traditionally flavoured with vanilla, although nowadays other flavourings, such as grated citrus zest, chocolate and liqueurs, are often added.
CREME MOUSSELINE: This is a crème pâtissière enriched with butter, used as a filling for sponge cakes and as a base for desserts. It is firmer than crème pâtissière, which is why it is used as a filling for the tiers of choux puffs in croquembouche (see page 12).
CREME PATISSIERE: A term used to describe a custard thickened with both plain flour and cornflour. It can be used as a base for soufflés, and as a filling for cakes, tarts and pastries – especially éclairs.

TRICK OF THE TRADE

IF A CUSTARD CURDLES

If the heat is too high when cooking a custard on top of the stove, it will separate and look curdled. To rescue it, remove the pan from the heat and beat with the spoon until blended. Another solution is to strain the custard through a fine sieve into a blender and work it until smooth. Reheat gently.

BATTERS

Many cooks lack confidence when it comes to making crêpes, pancakes and Yorkshire puddings, and yet there is no mystique about them. Follow the techniques shown here for smooth batters and successful results every time.

CREPE BATTER

125 g plain flour
½ tsp salt
2 eggs, beaten
300 ml milk or milk and water

Sift the flour and salt into a bowl, make a well in the centre and add the eggs. Gradually beat in the flour from the sides and slowly pour in the liquid to make a smooth batter. Sieve if necessary (see opposite page). Cover and let rest for 30 minutes or overnight. Beat thoroughly before using. Makes about 12 crêpes.

CREPE AND BLINI PANS

Crêpe and blini pans are made of cast iron, which conducts heat well and cooks food evenly. The only difference is the size – crêpe pans are usually 22 cm in diameter, blini pans 12 cm. Once the pan is "proved" or seasoned, it is practically non-stick. To prove, heat the pan and rub with salt. Wipe clean and repeat with oil. Do not wash the pan after use, just wipe it clean.

MAKING CREPES

French chefs use a special well-seasoned pan (see box, left) to make wafer-thin crêpes, but you can use a non-stick frying pan. Don't worry if the first few crêpes tear or stick. There are many elements to get right: the temperature of the pan, the temperature and amount of butter, and the consistency and amount of batter.

1 Put a knob of butter in the pan and heat over a moderate heat until foaming. Pour off the excess melted butter into a bowl, then pour in a small ladleful of batter, starting in the centre of the pan.

2 Tilt the pan to swirl the batter over the base and reach the edges, adding more batter if necessary.

3 Cook for about 1 minute until golden underneath and bubbles appear. Loosen and turn with a palette knife.

4 Cook the second side for 30 seconds–1 minute, then turn the crêpe out, first side facing down.

CIGARETTES

PANNEQUETS

FANS

MAKING YORKSHIRE PUDDINGS

For well-risen, crisp and light puddings, use very hot fat, otherwise the puddings will not rise.

Put about ¹/₂ tsp white vegetable fat or oil in each cup of a Yorkshire pudding tin and heat at 220°C until very hot, almost smoking. Pour in the batter and bake for 20–25 minutes.

YORKSHIRE PUDDING BATTER
Substitute strong plain flour for the plain flour in the original recipe – the extra gluten creates a more elastic batter, giving a better and more stable rise. Use a mixture of equal parts milk and water rather than all milk. The addition of the water will help to lighten the batter.

MAKING GRIDDLE PANCAKES

Traditional American pancakes are about 10 cm in diameter. Also popular are the fun-sized "silver dollars" shown here, so-called because of their shape. Like Scotch pancakes, they are about 5 cm in diameter. Make them on a griddle, or in a heavy-based frying pan. Test the temperature of the pan by sprinkling over a little water; it should sizzle and evaporate. Grease lightly before spooning on the batter.

1 Make the batter (see box right). Place tablespoons of batter on the hot griddle, spacing them well apart.

2 Cook until the edges are brown and the tops bubbling. Turn with a palette knife; cook until golden.

GRIDDLE PANCAKE BATTER
A thick batter is used for griddle pancakes because they need to hold their own shape as they cook unsupported on the griddle. Use 225 g plain flour (almost double the amount given in the crêpe batter recipe) to each 300 ml liquid and add 1–2 tbsp melted butter and 1–2 tsp baking powder. The butter will enrich the batter; the baking powder will aerate it.

TRICK OF THE TRADE

MAKING A SMOOTH BATTER

If making batter by hand, blend the flour and eggs with a balloon whisk for best results, and add the liquid gradually. If lumps occur, pour the batter through a sieve. For a foolproof method, work all the ingredients together in an electric blender there should be no need to sieve.

After making batter by hand, pass it through a fine-meshed sieve to ensure smoothness.

For an ultra-smooth batter, work the ingredients in an electric blender for 1 minute until smooth.

SHAPES FOR CREPES

For rolled or folded crêpes as shown on the opposite page, spread filling in centre, then proceed as follows:

- For cigarettes, fold in two opposite sides, then roll up from one of the other sides.
- For pannequets, fold in two opposite sides, then fold in the other sides and turn over.
- For fans, fold in half, then fold in half again.

CHOOSING & USING EGGS

Eggs are one of our most valued and useful ingredients in the kitchen – many recipes simply wouldn't be possible without their aerating, thickening and emulsifying capabilities.

FREE-RANGE

Around 85% of eggs in the UK are produced using the "laying cage system" or battery method. For eggs to be called free-range, the birds must have access to runs and a variety of vegetation, such as grass and corn. Although they have more freedom, these hens are more affected by weather conditions and predators and, as a result, they are a little more expensive.

SHELL COLOURS

The colour of an egg shell is determined by the breed of hen and its diet. The colour can range from speckled (quail's egg) to blue (duck's egg). Hen's eggs, either white or brown, are most commonly used – they taste the same, the difference in colour having no effect on flavour.

How to Test for Freshness

First check the "best before" date (see Safety First box, opposite page). If there is no date, test the freshness by immersing the egg in water as shown here. As the egg gets older it loses water through the shell, making the air pocket larger – so the older the egg the lighter it will be.

A fresh egg is heavy due to its high water content. It will settle horizontally on the bottom of the glass.

With a less fresh egg the air pockets will expand and make the egg float vertically, tip down, in the water.

An old, stale egg contains too much air and will float to the surface of the water. Do not use the egg.

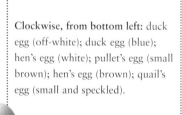

Clockwise, from bottom left: duck egg (off-white); duck egg (blue); hen's egg (white); pullet's egg (small brown); hen's egg (brown); quail's egg (small and speckled).

Separating Yolk from White

It is easiest to separate eggs when they are cold – the yolk is firm, and there is less chance that it will run into the white. Whites will not whisk properly if there is any yolk in them.

HAND METHOD
Crack egg into a bowl, then lift it up and cup it in your hand to let all the white drip through your fingers.

SHELL METHOD
Crack egg shell in half. Pass the yolk backwards and forwards between the halves until the white is in the bowl.

SAFETY FIRST

- Use eggs within the "best before" date. Check for the Lion Mark which ensures hygienic production standards greater than those required by UK or EC law.
- Salmonella bacteria can enter eggs through cracks in the shell, so only buy eggs with clean, undamaged shells.
- Wash your hands before and after handling egg shells.
- The elderly, people who are suffering an illness, pregnant women, babies and children are vulnerable to the risk of salmonella. All should avoid eating raw eggs and foods containing them.
- It is important to cook all egg dishes thoroughly – heat destroys salmonella.

TRICK OF THE TRADE

BLENDING ALBUMEN STRANDS

Egg yolk is anchored in the white by thick albumen strands. The strands should be sieved or blended into the whites so that they help to stabilize the foam.

SIEVING
Work the egg white through a fine sieve held over a bowl with a spoon to break up the albumen strands.

BLENDING
Put the egg whites in a bowl and use chopsticks or a fork to lift the whites and break up the albumen strands.

STORING EGGS

- Refrigerate eggs as soon as possible after buying them.
- Store eggs in their carton, away from strong-smelling foods.
- Store eggs pointed-end down to keep the yolks centred.
- Separated whites and yolks or shelled whole eggs should be refrigerated in airtight containers. Whites will keep for 1 week, yolks and whole eggs up to 2 days.
- Use food containing raw eggs within 2 days.
- Hard-boiled eggs in their shells will keep for up to 1 week.

NUTRITIONAL VALUE OF EGGS

Eggs are a valuable source of protein (one large egg contains 12–15% of the recommended daily allowance for an adult), supplying all essential amino acids needed by the body.

They also contain the minerals iron, iodine and calcium and vitamins A, B, D, E and K. Indeed, vitamin C is the only vitamin that is not present in an egg.

Eggs are also low in calories, supplying about 75 calories each. In the past, a limit on the number of eggs consumed per person per week was advised because of the cholesterol content, but more recent research shows that the dietary intake of saturated fat is the main cause of increased blood cholesterol levels. So, despite the fact that an egg contains 213 mg of cholesterol, all of which is within the yolk, the level of saturated fat is very low.

Although egg intake is restricted in some special diets, the current UK dietary guideline for egg consumption for an adult is 2–3 eggs per week.

WHISKING EGG WHITES

To achieve greater volume and stability before whisking egg whites, let them stand at room temperature for about 1 hour in a covered bowl. Whether whisking by hand or machine, make sure all utensils are free of grease and that the bowl is deep enough to hold the volume of whisked whites.

BY HAND

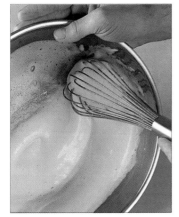

Put whites in a stainless steel or glass bowl. Whisk them from the bottom of the bowl upwards in a circular motion. For greatest volume, use a large balloon whisk.

BY MACHINE

With the whisk attachment of a tabletop electric mixer, start whisking slowly, to break up the whites, then increase the speed as they thicken. A little salt relaxes the albumen and makes whisking easier.

MAKING EGG WASH

A mixture of egg yolk and water is brushed over bread or pastry before baking to give a rich, golden colour and a glossy glaze.

Mix 1 egg yolk with 1 tbsp water and a pinch of salt. Whisk with a fork until combined. Brush the egg wash over bread or pastry with a pastry brush just before baking.

FINISHING TOUCHES

Great garnishes make simple desserts spectacular. The following are best made in advance so they will have time to set or dry. Imaginative chocolate shapes give cakes a professional touch. Drizzled caramel nests and crisp biscuits dress up parfaits, while tuile baskets can cradle ice cream or fruit. Use candied citrus zest to balance rich flavours.

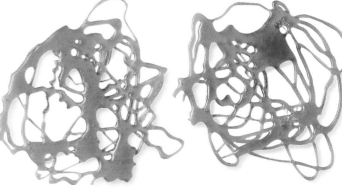

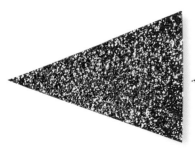

CHOCOLATE ROSE LEAVES
Wipe leaves with a damp tea towel; pat dry. Melt 300 g chocolate of your choice. Hold the leaf by the stem and brush a generous coating of chocolate on one side of the leaf – the underside gives best results. Refrigerate until firm, then gently peel the leaf away from the chocolate.

DRIZZLED CARAMEL SHAPES
Make a heavy sugar syrup, then cook to a caramel. Line a baking sheet with oiled baking parchment. Take a spoonful of caramel and drizzle it on to the parchment, letting it fall from the tip of the spoon. Let the shapes cool, then lift them off the paper.

DOUBLE-DUSTED CHOCOLATE
Make chocolate shapes. Put a little icing sugar in a sieve and gently tap it over the shapes. Put a little cocoa powder in another sieve and dust on top of the icing sugar. You can vary the effect by using cocoa powder first, or by dusting cocoa powder on white chocolate.

CHOCOLATE CURLS
Hold a block of room-temperature white or dark chocolate firmly and run a vegetable peeler along one edge to make curls. For best results, use chocolate with a low cocoa butter content or baker's chocolate, both of which are less likely to crack.

TUILE BASKETS

CHOCOLATE CIGARETTES

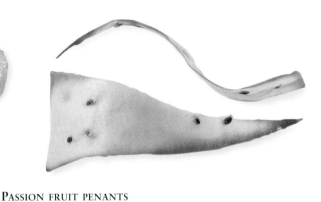

1 Make a stencil paste (see page 38). Line a baking sheet with baking parchment. Spread 1 tbsp paste in a sunburst shape.

2 Bake, four at a time, at 180°C until edges are golden, 5–8 minutes. Transfer to a bowl. Weight down with a biscuit cutter. Makes 16.

1 Spread 300 g tempered couverture chocolate over the back of a baking sheet. Once set, rub the chocolate's surface to warm it slightly.

2 Hold the baking sheet steady and slide a pastry scraper under the chocolate to form cigarette shapes. Makes about 30.

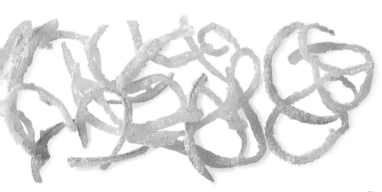

CANDIED LIME ZEST

PASSION FRUIT PENANTS

1 Cook blanched zest strips in a light sugar syrup, 10 minutes. Add 100 g sugar and simmer for 20 minutes. Drain and let set.

2 Once set, roll the zest in caster sugar and place on a sheet of baking parchment to harden.

1 Add 60 g passion fruit seeds to stencil paste (see page 38). Spread over stencil on baking parchment. Remove stencil; repeat.

2 Bake, six at a time, at 180°C until edges are golden, 5–8 minutes. Transfer shapes to an oiled rolling pin. Leave to set. Makes 12.

MEASUREMENT CHARTS

Accurate measurements are crucial to the success of any dish. The following charts give quick and easy reference for gauging oven temperatures and converting metric and imperial units for ingredients and equipment.

OVEN TEMPERATURES

CELSIUS	FAHRENHEIT	GAS	DESCRIPTION
110°C	225°F	¼	Cool
120°C	250°F	½	Cool
140°C	275°F	1	Very low
150°C	300°F	2	Very low
160°C	325°F	3	Low
170°C	325°F	3	Moderate
180°C	350°F	4	Moderate
190°C	375°F	5	Moderately hot
200°C	400°F	6	Hot
220°C	425°F	7	Hot
230°C	450°F	8	Very hot

US CUPS

CUPS	METRIC
¼ cup	60 ml
⅓ cup	70 ml
½ cup	125 ml
⅔ cup	150 ml
¾ cup	175 ml
1 cup	250 ml
1½ cups	375 ml
2 cups	500 ml
3 cups	750 ml
4 cups	1 litre
6 cups	1.5 litres

SPOONS

METRIC	IMPERIAL
1.25 ml	¼ tsp
2.5 ml	½ tsp
5 ml	1 tsp
10 ml	2 tsp
15 ml	3 tsp/1 tbsp
30 ml	2 tbsp
45 ml	3 tbsp
60 ml	4 tbsp
75 ml	5 tbsp
90 ml	6 tbsp

VOLUME

METRIC	IMPERIAL	METRIC	IMPERIAL	METRIC	IMPERIAL
25 ml	1 fl oz	300 ml	10 fl oz/½ pint	1 litre	1¾ pints
50 ml	2 fl oz	350 ml	12 fl oz	1.2 litres	2 pints
75 ml	2½ fl oz	400 ml	14 fl oz	1.3 litres	2¼ pints
100 ml	3½ fl oz	425 ml	15 fl oz/¾ pint	1.4 litres	2½ pints
125 ml	4 fl oz	450 ml	16 fl oz	1.5 litres	2¾ pints
150 ml	5 fl oz/¼ pint	500 ml	18 fl oz	1.7 litres	3 pints
175 ml	6 fl oz	568 ml	20 fl oz/1 pint	2 litres	3½ pints
200 ml	7 fl oz/⅓ pint	600 ml	1 pint milk	2.5 litres	4½ pints
225 ml	8 fl oz	700 ml	1¼ pints	2.8 litres	5 pints
250 ml	9 fl oz	850 ml	1½ pints	3 litres	5¼ pints

WEIGHT

METRIC	IMPERIAL	METRIC	IMPERIAL
5 g	⅛ oz	325 g	11½ oz
10 g	¼ oz	350 g	12 oz
15 g	½ oz	375 g	13 oz
20 g	¾ oz	400 g	14 oz
25 g	1 oz	425 g	15 oz
35 g	1¼ oz	450 g	1 lb
40 g	1½ oz	500 g	1 lb 2 oz
50 g	1¾ oz	550 g	1 lb 4 oz
55 g	2 oz	600 g	1 lb 5 oz
60 g	2¼ oz	650 g	1 lb 7 oz
70 g	2½ oz	700 g	1 lb 9 oz
75 g	2¾ oz	750 g	1 lb 10 oz
85 g	3 oz	800 g	1 lb 12 oz
90 g	3¼ oz	850 g	1 lb 14 oz
100 g	3½ oz	900 g	2 lb
115 g	4 oz	950 g	2 lb 2 oz
125 g	4½ oz	1 kg	2 lb 4 oz
140 g	5 oz	1.25 kg	2 lb 12 oz
150 g	5½ oz	1.3 kg	3 lb
175 g	6 oz	1.5 kg	3 lb 5 oz
200 g	7 oz	1.6 kg	3 lb 8 oz
225 g	8 oz	1.8 kg	4 lb
250 g	9 oz	2 kg	4 lb 8 oz
275 g	9¾ oz	2.25 kg	5 lb
280 g	10 oz	2.5 kg	5 lb 8 oz
300 g	10½ oz	2.7 kg	6 lb
315 g	11 oz	3 kg	6 lb 8 oz

LINEAR MEASUREMENTS

METRIC	IMPERIAL	METRIC	IMPERIAL
2 mm	1⁄16 in	17 cm	6½ in
3 mm	⅛ in	18 cm	7 in
5 mm	¼ in	19 cm	7½ in
8 mm	⅜ in	20 cm	8 in
10 mm/1 cm	½ in	22 cm	8½ in
1.5 cm	⅝ in	23 cm	9 in
2 cm	¾ in	24 cm	9½ in
2.5 cm	1 in	25 cm	10 in
3 cm	1¼ in	26 cm	10½ in
4 cm	1½ in	27 cm	10¾ in
4.5 cm	1¾ in	28 cm	11 in
5 cm	2 in	29 cm	11½ in
5.5 cm	2¼ in	30 cm	12 in
6 cm	2½ in	31 cm	12½ in
7 cm	2¾ in	33 cm	13 in
7.5 cm	3 in	34 cm	13½ in
8 cm	3¼ in	35 cm	14 in
9 cm	3½ in	37 cm	14½ in
9.5 cm	3¾ in	38 cm	15 in
10 cm	4 in	39 cm	15½ in
11 cm	4¼ in	40 cm	16 in
12 cm	4½ in	42 cm	16½ in
12.5 cm	4¾ in	43 cm	17 in
13 cm	5 in	44 cm	17½ in
14 cm	5½ in	46 cm	18 in
15 cm	6 in	48 cm	19 in
16 cm	6¼ in	50 cm	20 in

INDEX